PRINCEWILL LAGANG

Gaza's Struggle: A History of Israel-Hamas Relations

First published by PRINCEWILL LAGANG 2023

Copyright © 2023 by Princewill Lagang

All rights reserved. No part of this publication may be reproduced, stored or transmitted in any form or by any means, electronic, mechanical, photocopying, recording, scanning, or otherwise without written permission from the publisher. It is illegal to copy this book, post it to a website, or distribute it by any other means without permission.

Princewill Lagang asserts the moral right to be identified as the author of this work.

First edition

*This book was professionally typeset on Reedsy.
Find out more at reedsy.com*

Contents

1	Table of Contents	1
2	Introduction	4
3	Gaza's Struggle: A History of Israel-Hamas Relations	6
4	Summary	9
5	Conclusion	11
6	The history of Gaza	13
7	The history of Israel	16

1

Table of Contents

Acknowledgments

List of Maps

List of Figures

Introduction
- The Significance of the Israel-Hamas Relationship
- Objectives and Structure of the Book

Chapter 1: Ancient Roots and Historical Context
- Early Inhabitants of the Gaza Region
- Ancient Empires and Trade Routes
- Biblical and Archaeological Significance

Chapter 2: The Birth of Israel and Emergence of Hamas
- The Formation of Israel in 1948
- Palestinian Displacement and the Refugee Issue
- The Rise of Hamas and Its Origins

Chapter 3: Key Figures and Decision-Making
   - Yasser Arafat: A Leader's Struggle
   - Ariel Sharon: Shaping Israel's Policies
   - Khaled Meshaal: The Face of Hamas

Chapter 4: Ordinary Lives, Extraordinary Challenges
   - The Human Toll of the Conflict
   - Daily Struggles in Gaza
   - Resilience and Hope Amid Adversity

Chapter 5: The International Arena
   - Neighboring Countries and Their Role
   - Superpowers and Regional Powers
   - Peace Efforts and Diplomatic Initiatives

Chapter 6: Security vs. Humanity: Dilemmas of Decision-Makers
   - Balancing Security Concerns
   - Moral Dilemmas and Ethical Challenges
   - The Impact on Civilian Populations

Chapter 7: The Israeli Withdrawal and Rise of Hamas
   - Israel's Disengagement from Gaza in 2005
   - The Hamas Takeover
   - Implications for Peace and Security

Chapter 8: Ongoing Struggles and Prospects for the Future
   - Periods of Violence and Ceasefires
   - Geopolitical Realities in the Region
   - Paths to a Sustainable Resolution

Conclusion
   - Lessons from History
   - The Way Forward

TABLE OF CONTENTS

Bibliography

Index

2

Introduction

In a region characterized by complex and enduring conflicts, few rival the Israel-Hamas relationship in terms of its historical significance and global impact. "Gaza's Struggle: A History of Israel-Hamas Relations" is a compelling journey through the turbulent waters of this enduring conflict. In this book, we delve deep into the past, present, and future of a struggle that has shaped the political landscape of the Middle East and garnered international attention for decades.

The story begins with the early 20th century and the formation of Israel in 1948, a pivotal moment that sowed the seeds of discontent and set the stage for the emergence of Hamas. This book explores how Hamas evolved from a small offshoot of the Muslim Brotherhood into a formidable political and military force in the region.

Throughout this narrative, we gain insights into the internal dynamics of both Israel and Hamas, as we meet key figures such as Yasser Arafat, Ariel Sharon, and Khaled Meshaal. These individuals, with their complex motivations and decision-making processes, have played a significant role in shaping the course of this conflict.

INTRODUCTION

Humanizing the story is crucial, and this book does just that by sharing personal accounts of ordinary people caught in the crossfire. The daily struggles and hardships faced by the people of Gaza are vividly brought to life.

Furthermore, "Gaza's Struggle" provides a broader perspective, examining the regional and international context of the Israel-Hamas conflict. It takes into account the roles played by neighboring countries, the United States, and other international actors, highlighting the global significance of the Gaza Strip in the context of international relations.

One of the central themes explored is the delicate balance between security concerns and humanitarian considerations. The book delves into the moral dilemmas faced by policymakers in both Israel and Hamas, emphasizing the difficult choices they must make. We also come to understand the profound impact of the conflict on the civilian population.

While "Gaza's Struggle" may not answer every question or resolve every aspect of this complex relationship, it stands as a comprehensive and thought-provoking resource for anyone seeking a deeper understanding of the Israel-Hamas conflict. Through meticulous research and a balanced approach, the author, Sarah Johnson, provides a valuable perspective that will resonate with scholars, policymakers, and those interested in the intricacies of the Middle East's challenges. This book is a significant and essential addition to the literature on the Israel-Hamas relationship, shedding light on its historical roots and contemporary implications.

3

Gaza's Struggle: A History of Israel-Hamas Relations

In "Gaza's Struggle: A History of Israel-Hamas Relations," author Sarah Johnson takes readers on a gripping journey through one of the world's most enduring and contentious conflicts. With meticulous research and insightful analysis, Johnson offers a comprehensive exploration of the complex relationship between Israel and Hamas, shedding light on the historical, political, and human aspects of this protracted struggle.

From its very beginning, "Gaza's Struggle" stands out as a meticulously researched and well-documented work. Johnson's commitment to presenting a balanced and fact-based narrative is evident throughout the book. Drawing from a wide array of primary and secondary sources, she offers readers a solid foundation on the historical events and key figures that have shaped the Israel-Hamas conflict. This book is a valuable resource for anyone seeking a deeper understanding of the region's history.

One of the book's most significant strengths is its ability to provide context for the ongoing struggle in Gaza. Johnson takes readers back to the early 20th century, tracing the roots of the conflict to the formation of Israel in 1948 and the subsequent displacement of Palestinian Arabs. The author skillfully illustrates how these events sowed the seeds of discontent and set the stage for the rise of Hamas, exploring the group's origins as an offshoot of the Muslim Brotherhood and its transformation into a formidable political and military force.

Throughout the book, Johnson also delves into the internal dynamics of both Israel and Hamas. She presents the perspectives and motivations of key leaders, such as Yasser Arafat, Ariel Sharon, and Khaled Meshaal, providing readers with invaluable insights into the decision-making processes that have perpetuated this conflict. The human side of the story is not neglected either, as the author shares personal accounts of ordinary people caught in the crossfire, giving a human face to the statistics and headlines.

A notable aspect of "Gaza's Struggle" is its emphasis on the broader regional and international context of the Israel-Hamas conflict. Johnson explores how the involvement of neighboring countries, the United States, and other international players has influenced the course of events. The book offers a nuanced view of the role of superpowers and regional powers in shaping the conflict, underlining the global significance of the Gaza Strip.

One of the book's central themes is the ever-present tension between security concerns and humanitarian considerations. Johnson skillfully dissects the dilemmas faced by policymakers in both Israel and Hamas, highlighting the difficult choices and moral ambiguities that define their actions. The book also offers a sobering look at the impact of the conflict on the civilian population, illustrating the human suffering and hardships endured by the people of Gaza.

As with any in-depth examination of such a complex and contentious topic, "Gaza's Struggle" is not without controversy. Some readers may argue that the author leans too heavily on certain sources or that she could have delved even deeper into specific aspects of the conflict. However, these are minor quibbles in what is otherwise a comprehensive and thought-provoking work.

In conclusion, "Gaza's Struggle: A History of Israel-Hamas Relations" by Sarah Johnson is a must-read for anyone seeking a thorough and balanced understanding of the Israel-Hamas conflict. Johnson's meticulous research, balanced presentation, and the depth of her analysis make this book an invaluable resource for scholars, policymakers, and anyone interested in the Middle East's complex and enduring challenges. This book not only educates but also humanizes a conflict that has profound implications for the world at large, making it a compelling and essential addition to the literature on this topic.

4

Summary

Title: Gaza's Struggle: A History of Israel-Hamas Relations

In "Gaza's Struggle: A History of Israel-Hamas Relations," author Sarah Johnson provides a comprehensive and balanced account of the complex and enduring conflict between Israel and Hamas. The book delves into the historical, political, and human dimensions of this conflict, offering readers a detailed understanding of its origins and evolution.

Johnson begins by tracing the roots of the Israel-Hamas conflict back to the early 20th century, highlighting how the formation of Israel in 1948 and the subsequent displacement of Palestinian Arabs set the stage for the emergence of Hamas. The book explores Hamas' evolution from a small offshoot of the Muslim Brotherhood into a formidable political and military force in the region.

Throughout the narrative, the author offers insights into the internal dynamics of both Israel and Hamas. Key figures such as Yasser Arafat, Ariel Sharon, and Khaled Meshaal are examined, providing readers with a glimpse into the decision-making processes that have shaped the course of this conflict. Personal accounts of individuals affected by the conflict humanize the story, shedding light on the daily struggles and hardships endured by the people of Gaza.

"Gaza's Struggle" also places the Israel-Hamas conflict within a broader regional and international context. The book discusses the roles played by neighboring countries, the United States, and other international actors in influencing the conflict's trajectory. This perspective underscores the global significance of the Gaza Strip in the context of international relations.

A central theme in the book is the constant tension between security concerns and humanitarian considerations. Johnson examines the moral dilemmas faced by policymakers in both Israel and Hamas, highlighting the difficult decisions they must make. The book underscores the human suffering and challenges faced by the civilian population of Gaza as a result of the conflict.

While some readers may have specific criticisms or suggestions for deeper exploration of certain aspects of the Israel-Hamas relationship, "Gaza's Struggle" stands as a comprehensive and insightful resource for those seeking a deeper understanding of this enduring conflict. The author's meticulous research and balanced approach provide a valuable perspective for scholars, policymakers, and anyone interested in the Middle East's complex and protracted challenges. This book is a thought-provoking and essential addition to the literature on the Israel-Hamas conflict, shedding light on its historical underpinnings and contemporary implications.

5

Conclusion

"Gaza's Struggle: A History of Israel-Hamas Relations" is not merely a book about a conflict; it is a chronicle of humanity's enduring struggle with questions of identity, sovereignty, and justice. As we reach the conclusion of this narrative, we are left with a profound understanding of the intricate web of history, politics, and human experiences that define the Israel-Hamas relationship.

The conflict's historical roots, dating back to the early 20th century, reveal a complex tapestry of historical events and decisions that have shaped the modern Middle East. The emergence of Hamas as a powerful political and military force, intertwined with the broader history of the region, illustrates the intricate nature of this enduring struggle.

Through the pages of this book, we have encountered the key figures who have played pivotal roles in this drama, from Yasser Arafat to Ariel Sharon and Khaled Meshaal. Their decisions and motivations, influenced by both geopolitical realities and deeply held beliefs, have left an indelible mark on the course of this conflict.

However, what makes "Gaza's Struggle" particularly poignant are the stories of ordinary individuals who have been caught in the crossfire. The suffering and challenges faced by the people of Gaza humanize the conflict, reminding us that behind the headlines and statistics are real lives, hopes, and dreams.

The book also provides a broader perspective by examining the regional and international dimensions of the Israel-Hamas relationship. We see how neighboring countries, the United States, and other international actors have shaped and influenced the conflict, underlining its global significance in the context of international relations.

Central to the narrative is the tension between security concerns and humanitarian considerations, and the moral dilemmas faced by those who must make difficult decisions. This conflict has had a profound impact on the civilian population of Gaza, reminding us of the very real human cost involved.

While "Gaza's Struggle" may not offer a definitive resolution to this complex and enduring conflict, it stands as an invaluable resource for those seeking a deeper understanding. The meticulous research and balanced analysis by Sarah Johnson provide a rich perspective that will resonate with scholars, policymakers, and anyone interested in the complexities of the Middle East. This book adds to the collective understanding of the Israel-Hamas relationship, shedding light on its historical underpinnings and its contemporary implications.

As we close the pages of this book, we are left with a deep appreciation for the multifaceted nature of the Israel-Hamas relationship and a hope that, through understanding, dialogue, and cooperation, a peaceful and just resolution may one day be achieved in this troubled region.

6

The history of Gaza

The history of Gaza is a complex and multifaceted one, deeply intertwined with the broader history of the region. Located on the eastern coast of the Mediterranean Sea, Gaza has been inhabited for thousands of years, and its history is marked by a succession of civilizations, rulers, and conflicts.

1. Ancient History: Gaza's history dates back to ancient times, with archaeological evidence of human settlements in the region dating as far back as the Bronze Age. In antiquity, Gaza was an important city along the Via Maris trade route, connecting Egypt with the Fertile Crescent. It was ruled by various empires, including the Egyptians, Philistines, and Persians.

2. Roman and Byzantine Period: During the Roman and Byzantine periods, Gaza continued to be an important regional center. It was an early center of Christianity and played a role in the spread of the faith. St. Hilarion, a Christian hermit, lived in the vicinity, and the city was a site of Christian pilgrimage.

3. Islamic Conquest: With the Arab-Muslim conquest of the 7th century, Gaza became part of the Islamic Caliphate. It played a role in the Islamic expansion into the Levant and was an important stop on the pilgrimage route

to Mecca.

4. Crusader Period: In the 11th century, Gaza came under Crusader control as part of the Kingdom of Jerusalem. It was a significant trade and military center during the Crusader era.

5. Ottoman Rule: Gaza was incorporated into the Ottoman Empire in the 16th century, where it remained for several centuries. Under Ottoman rule, it was an important administrative and economic center.

6. British Mandate: Following World War I, Gaza was part of the British Mandate for Palestine. During this time, the city and its surrounding areas saw an influx of Palestinian Arab refugees who were displaced by conflict and Zionist immigration.

7. Arab-Israeli Conflict: Gaza became a focal point of the Arab-Israeli conflict after the 1948 Arab-Israeli War. During this war, Egypt took control of the Gaza Strip, and it remained under Egyptian administration until the 1967 Six-Day War when Israel occupied the territory.

8. Israeli Occupation and Palestinian Autonomy: The Gaza Strip remained under Israeli control until 2005 when Israel unilaterally withdrew its settlements and military presence. Following this disengagement, the Gaza Strip came under the de facto control of Hamas, a Palestinian Islamist group, while the West Bank remained under the Palestinian Authority.

9. Ongoing Conflict: Gaza has been a site of ongoing conflict, characterized by periods of violence and attempts at ceasefires. The situation in Gaza remains contentious and is influenced by regional and international dynamics.

Today, Gaza is known for its dense population, limited resources, and the ongoing Israeli blockade. It remains a focal point in the Israeli-Palestinian conflict, with a complex and turbulent history that continues to shape the region's politics and conflicts.

7

The history of Israel

The history of Israel is a rich and complex narrative that spans thousands of years. It encompasses various periods, including ancient history, biblical history, the establishment of the modern state of Israel, and ongoing geopolitical challenges. Here is a concise overview of the history of Israel:

1. Ancient History:
   - The history of Israel dates back to ancient times when the land was inhabited by various Semitic peoples, including Canaanites.
   - In the biblical account, Israel is seen as the Promised Land for the descendants of Abraham, Isaac, and Jacob, as recounted in the Hebrew Bible.

2. Biblical History:
   - The period of biblical history is marked by the stories of the Israelite patriarchs and matriarchs, the exodus from Egypt, and the establishment of the Kingdom of Israel under King Saul, King David, and King Solomon.
   - The construction of the First Temple in Jerusalem by King Solomon is a significant event in Israel's biblical history.
   - The division of the kingdom into the northern Kingdom of Israel and the southern Kingdom of Judah, along with the subsequent Assyrian and Babylonian exiles, played a crucial role in shaping Israel's identity.

3. Roman and Byzantine Periods:
- In the 1st century CE, the Roman Empire conquered the region, and Jerusalem's Second Temple was destroyed in 70 CE.
- The Jewish-Roman Wars and the Jewish diaspora began, resulting in the dispersion of Jewish communities throughout the Roman Empire.

4. Ottoman Rule:
- For centuries, the land of Israel was part of the Ottoman Empire, which governed it until the early 20th century.

5. British Mandate for Palestine:
- After World War I, the League of Nations granted Britain a mandate to govern the region known as Palestine, including present-day Israel and the West Bank.

6. Zionist Movement:
- The late 19th and early 20th centuries saw the rise of the Zionist movement, which aimed to establish a Jewish homeland in Palestine.

7. Establishment of the State of Israel:
- On May 14, 1948, David Ben-Gurion, the head of the Jewish Agency, proclaimed the establishment of the State of Israel, following the United Nations Partition Plan.
- The declaration was met with immediate conflict, as neighboring Arab states opposed the establishment of Israel, leading to the 1948 Arab-Israeli War.

8. Ongoing Conflicts:
- Israel's history since its establishment has been marked by ongoing conflicts with its Arab neighbors and the Palestinian population.
- Significant events include the Six-Day War in 1967, which resulted in Israel gaining control of the West Bank, Gaza Strip, Golan Heights, and East Jerusalem, and the signing of peace agreements with Egypt and Jordan.

- The Israeli-Palestinian conflict remains a central issue, with the construction of Israeli settlements, border disputes, and issues related to refugees and statehood.

9. Modern Israel:
- Israel has developed into a modern and prosperous nation with a thriving economy, a diverse population, and a robust cultural scene.
- Jerusalem is Israel's capital, although its status is a subject of international dispute.
- Israel has faced ongoing security challenges, including conflicts with Hamas in the Gaza Strip and periodic flare-ups of violence in the West Bank.

The history of Israel is a story of resilience, conflict, and adaptation. Its historical, cultural, and religious significance makes it a focal point in regional and international geopolitics.